A MILLION
IN PRIZES

New Issues Poetry & Prose

Editor	William Olsen
Managing Editor	Marianne Swierenga
Copy Editor	Kory M. Shrum
Assistant Editors	Adam Clay & Kimberly Kolbe
Readers	Matt Browning, Natalie Giarratano, Alison Laurell, Michael Levan, Gary McDowell, Rebecah Pulsifer, Cindy St. John, Laura Zawistowski

New Issues Poetry & Prose
The College of Arts and Sciences
Western Michigan University
Kalamazoo, MI 49008

Copyright © 2009 by Justin Marks. All rights reserved.
Printed in the United States of America.

First Edition, 2009.

ISBN-10   1-930974-81-7 (paperbound)
ISBN-13   978-1-930974-81-4 (paperbound)

Library of Congress Cataloging-in-Publication Data:
Marks, Justin
A Million in Prizes/Justin Marks
Library of Congress Control Number: 2008938518

Art Director	Tricia Hennessy
Designer	NatalieAnn Rich
Production Manager	Paul Sizer
	The Design Center, Frostic School of Art
	College of Fine Arts
	Western Michigan University

A MILLION
IN PRIZES

JUSTIN MARKS

New Issues

WESTERN MICHIGAN UNIVERSITY

In Memoriam
Janice Rothery Marks

Contents

Acknowledgements:

Grateful acknowledgement to the following journals in which versions of these poems first appeared, some under different titles:

Absent: The Detonator Always Has a Red Button
Bedside Guide to No Tell Motel, Second Floor: The Split Ends of My Beard Have Split Ends
Black Warrior Review: Home Again
Cannibal: *Cédez Le Pasage*, Last Year's Model
The Cultural Society: Further Down the Purchase Funnel, Settling In
Essays & Fictions: Another Year of My Life With Me, False Teeth, Present Whereabouts Unknown
Handsome: A Million In Prizes
horse less review: selections from [Summer   insular]
Kulture Vulture: No More Antecedents
The Literary Review: Childhood
Melancholia's Tremulous Dreadlocks: Matter of Fact
New York Quarterly: Sea to Sea
Typo: Little Happier
Word For / Word: Mantra, On the Making of Things

[Summer   insular] appeared as a chapbook from horse less press in 2007

For keen editorial eyes, love, support and friendship, I owe many thanks to: Dan Boehl, Ana Božičević, Elisa Gabbert, Tom Lisk, Sampson Starkweather, Janaka Stucky, Chris Tonelli, my family and, above all, Meridith Rohana.

Life Is Elsewhere

Matter of Fact

I wanted to create the ocean, the sky,
the intricate structure of a leaf

and thought by now
I'd have come close.

What joy I have in knowing
creation of that sort

doesn't exist.
The world has little

use for me.
Its glare blinds.

How glad I am
for the orbit I inhabit.

A planet to the sun.

Childhood

I was afraid of what lay beyond
the snowball bush that separated
the backyard from the woods.
My memory—mostly light
specks of white afloat in space—
is spotty. I had a vivid sense that
things prowled out there I should fear.
I tried to go into the woods once,
didn't make it more than a few
steps when suddenly I heard
myself yell, *help!*
sure I was lost as I ran across
the yard to my mother. She tried
to tell me I was fine,
that it was all OK, but couldn't help
laughing at how easily I scared.
The shame I felt then
is the shame I have now, though tempered
by my healthy adult knowledge
that I was just a kid. I hated
being a child. My shame
is having been one at all.
Since then, I've been cultivating
an ability to look back on myself
as someone other than myself. Better yet,
no one at all. Instead, a mere body

moving through space under some other
volition, like lights from far off cars—sudden
shapes in shapeless nights—going down a road
at the edge of a field outside a bedroom window
each night, their headlights pointing to where
no one cares as long as they are gone soon.

Little Happier

All that whiteness was still before me,
a field of snow on which
not one foot seemed to have left a print.
Around the field, cold and rickety trees,
their shadows hovering
as if they were not shadows but shade,
independent of what cast their image
on the ground. It was as if
there were no tree . . . whiteness without end,
but touched with such shading as needed
to keep things interesting.

Looking closer,
foot paths and sometimes roads appeared
and it was a different season,
or maybe as subtle as
a few minutes later,
the world still orbiting
the sun endlessly adjusting the shadows—
a little to the left; there, now up a bit.

One year I forgot
to spray the budding
little apple tree in the backyard.
From then on worms
each year more freely preyed
on it so tenderly grown,
which reminded me that that tree really exists,
as do others.

And I am aware of my legs
that lift me from this chair

and set me down,
arms and hands that carry things,
make for my chin a place to rest.
And those trees like constant elbows
to my ribs.

Thank you
for making me think like this,
and worse yet, making me see
how much I enjoy it,
how naïve I was to say,
whiteness without end.

Settling In

Vague traffic sounds outside the window.
A light snow falling. Waking a little.
Slipping off again. The distinctions

between things blurring not to the point
of being indistinguishable, but softening
the parts of myself normally barred

from each other. More than where
public and private selves merge,
here is where the selves I might

become are cast on
those I've been. Here is where
one learns to lay claim to nothing.

I wake, my not-yet-self
projecting back on the life I rise into.

Sea to Sea

Thirty-seven thousand feet up. Below,
the Midwest's patchwork plots
of land conspire to form and formlessness.

At the line where sky and land meet
the air gets grainy, as if seen through
the fine mesh of mosquito net.

Pieces of my life, those same old things,
come around again
as memory, as this moment,
as things to neither trust nor mistrust.

Perhaps it would have been better
if I didn't say anything.
A painter I know said once,
Silence is so accurate . . .

A little turbulence. Engines nearly inaudible.
A clear plastic cup on my tray table.
Cold water almost perfectly still.

After the Money's Gone

The last time
I was in a bar
everyone was drinking
a brand of beer
I'd never heard of.
I'd had too much
coffee. Blood
had been issuing
from places it shouldn't.
I was not a child anymore.
I'd just read that proof
of god's existence
would lead to scientific
proposals guaranteed
to get funded.
The night I got stuck
at a friend's house in a blizzard
and we took acid and dove
off his deck into several
feet of snow
was beyond belief.
The only fun I have now
is when I'm alone.
I Google myself,
and I'm a racecar driver.
There has always been
the problem of what to do
with my arms,
and never having
the appropriate clothes.
The music was
so loud,
and it wasn't even close
to last call.

No More Antecedents

I keep thinking
there's something I have

to go home for
There's not

So
I go on

trying to name
this non-home

which leaves me
with little

that's better than nothing
It's not the end

Mantra

Terrycloth sun setting over
the old steel-wool river

The air a translucent sphere of frayed
twine

The truth can be so lame

    Shifting forms
unchanging   My hands

know what they're doing—

On the Making of Things

You must occupy places. You must be alone. You must be
a surgeon specializing in amputations, on yourself, on others.

You must be a prosthetic, for yourself and others. You must be
and not be many things as much as possible.

Know that no one will ever love or hate you as much as you
already do.

Life Is Elsewhere

Looking out the window of a plane
at night, I'm filled with that
romantic feeling. The lights below
are indecipherable
letters of some unuttered language.
Nothing new. I'm sick
of the selves I've been.
Their gestures are all
I can conjure, a kind of
dishonesty, but one
that keeps me busy.
I was free
from disappointment
until I looked to the past
and thought: now what?
Trying to visualize
ten dimensions at once,
understanding reality as different
than it's already unknown to be—
a form of magic. Do you see
the difficulty? I'm delusional
when I sleep. It's better
to keep your eyes open.
The best time on earth
is one you don't remember.

[Summer   insular]

Summer   insular
season in which

the mind functions
as in no other

yet I've never
given myself over

to   I'm giving over
to now   in a way

but I can't
be sure

(I haven't done this before)
of much more

than what I've done
so far

which is a bit
more than I'd done before

I noticed the days getting longer
and warm   then hot

nature's   the city's
abundance in full bloom

Rain   Not much
Not for long

Technically
according to the calendar

it's still spring
May   and the weather

I admit
from time to time

agrees   Not summer
yet   not really

but most day . . .
Yesterday

I saw a video of
a volcano erupting

followed by long
shots of the aftermath

volcanic rock
formations in the ocean

all manner
of tropical fish and other

aquatic life obliviously swimming
as if landscape without a human

audience has no meaning
Without footage of the volcano

the underwater sequences
would merely have been pretty

And likely all
that will be left

when we finally
go extinct:

animals roaming round
our wreckage

no one to impose the passing
of one season to the next

I have to stop
thinking

lest I freak myself out   *man*
and fall into that thinking in which

nothing is possible
Stop

No help we can't
provide for ourselves

And what is there
to love about each other

but our stories
the ones we've made

might make
what we've left to imagine

I've written out that Roethke poem, folded it and placed it in my pocket. Should I die, it will be found on me, and that, aside from the fact that I will be dead, might mean something.

One painting: a bare
black tree pressed

into
black canvas

And you
I know you

That is
I know what you seem

to be   these
assumptions on my part

that what I say is worth
anything

to you
whom I have not

likely won't ever
meet

in person anyway
Now I must be getting on

with what I've got to get
(am going) to

A poem about summer
should be happy   right?

Summer is life
in full swing

leaves at their greenest
new animals taking their first

steps to independence
But to see   to try to see

some significance
into   I mean onto   things

I return to certain habits of mind
which are part of what I want

but not all   Happiness
for example   is lacking

taking a different
dinghy for a row

enjoying
a good smoke

Eat   Stare at a computer
screen   Some of what I do

to face the dead time
of each day

(to face
the day)

see myself
through to home

the books
the lying

out of myself
(the attempts to)

on these pages—
A life lived largely

in   I mean of
spare moments

I am aware
from whom I borrow

(steal outright)
and don't

No need
to name names

Another painting:
six large shoreline rocks

no shore
no sea

I have few
if any

allegiances
to place

I like it here
that pigeon

neck bent
cleaning its wing

on the fire escape rail
neighborhood kids

gathered on the corner—
where else

These negotiations
between the mind and what it sees . . .

the mind having little else
to see   to exert its energies on

except itself—
regardless of what its gaze falls on—

sees mainly itself
that is

creates a space
it labors to fill

voices
sound in

Today
stronger than usual

(which isn't that strong
but enough to allow me

to move through the day
with some cheer)

I feel good
like I'm right

to see things in rudiments
basic facts: outside

it is hot and sunny
a nice breeze blowing

In here
the cat sleeps

in front of the air conditioner
soundly   It's quiet   I'm

at ease (even if
uneasy about that)

The connections between
things occur

become apparent
instead of being

sought out
then shaken

down for all I think
they should yield

I'm finding the fissures
in things I've been looking for

places to squeeze
myself into

(Or do I mean onto)
Today is merely a day

lacking   like all days
the distance of history

the meanings and definitions
attached to it at the end

of an as-yet-undetermined
period of moving along

The end is not near
(not today   at least)

Nor a new
beginning

Little but preparing
for tomorrow is getting done

which somehow is enough
for today   it seems

I've always clung
to things—

ideas   crumpled up
pieces of paper   love   whatever

Human nature
is absolute

insistence
on mediocrity

most of us
too lazy

to be the awful
people we are

or the kinder folks
we could be

Trying
to be oneself

honestly
finding the words

allowing their arrival
arriving at them

easily
a life's worth of work

Word from the bosses today:
three weeks to improve

or they'll (be forced to) let me go
which   in truth   wouldn't

be all bad—more time
to sleep   write   eat   read   fuck—

except for having
of course   no income

A rainy summer day
Dark   the whole bit

(good sleeping weather)
Home

A kiss from Meri
another   more

then sex
a nap

Now she's making dinner
talking on the phone with the folks back home

(Dad's heart getting better
Stepmom's troubles staying

off the bottle)
For dessert:

pear gelato flecked
with flakes of chocolate

. . . coming out of
vanishing into . . .

At work today
I tried to be a good employee

get everything done correct
on time   stay focused

follow through
Participated in

office chatter
Made a joke even

That place   if it must
can have my time

my full attention
(from nine-to-five)

No place else
will have me

Summer
is nearly over

Time
for a good cry

Rise
babyface

Rain again   A Rainy summer
Mild as well   Have only

needed the air-conditioner
I'd say half the time

which has been nice
but this rain—

rain rain rain rain
rain rain rain rain

rain rain rain rain
rain rain rain rain—

is getting old
I have a hole in the sole

of my right shoe
which the water gets through

and goes squish squish squish
all day long

Down the shore for the weekend
(Ocean City   New Jersey)

by bus   Sun through
lightly-smeared windows

No one
next to me

Stretched out
read   slept a little

and now
watered and well fed

cloud cover crossing
the setting sun

I sing a little song to myself:
There's a cool breeze blowing

from off the shore
Got my girl by my side

We're sitting on the porch
watching the evening tide

Happiness out on the surf—
ride   ride   ride

Back home   A Sunday
Lounging

on the fire escape
Sun hot on the back

of my neck
October

But here   three floors up
moderate levels

of activity   traffic
a store front

radio tuned to the oldies
traces of summer

sluggishness—
what to do now

The Voice Inside
the Cheerleader's Megaphone

A Million In Prizes

That car is going to hit me I thought and
then it did and I wondered how it would
all turn out as the car screeched to a halt
and I rolled off the hood and the driver
came out telling the person on the other
end of her phone *I hit someone I gotta go
Oh my god hun Are you ok Oh your poor
knee Oh I'm sorry* A woman in a passing
car shouted *She ran a red light* Someone
walking by offered to get me a chair from
the corner sushi shop and be a witness
The chef said *You bring chair back* The
EMT said *Your heart rate is low* I was
peeing in a bottle at the hospital when a
guy was brought in who'd been hit by a
semi-truck but was moving his fingers I
heard the doctors say and then he was
dead *We're here for such a short time* the
nurse said as she took my urine and I
was taken for x-rays where it was revealed
I'd only suffered a small fracture and I
was brought back and sat in a wheelchair
and given a wooden cane which I would
later get many compliments on as it
made me look debonair people said A
bewildered looking priest was asking the
night nurse sorting the dead man's
personal effects whom he was here to
console as I was being wheeled to the
door where I was lucky enough to catch a
cab willing to take me the very short
distance home

The Detonator Always Has a Red Button

I am merely one to whom things happen. Being a child of the country, mosquitoes harassed me all the long summer nights.

What's most important to me now is water, my complexion, and urinating. In bed last night, I kept my genitals to myself.

I was going to say something about the clouds, these brand new clouds. Now I'm tempted to see where a round of drinks before every decision will take me.

When people discover my rural roots, they inevitably resort to calling me Huckleberry. The day crawls by like a living document, the prettier for having forgotten me.

Cédez Le Pasage

My stomach is not a calm, motionless Ziploc bag filled with liquid. As major life transactions continue to accumulate, human emotions make their presence increasingly known. Their sadness is all I can bear.

There are those who imagine heaven as a socialist state. I grew up without belief. Warm bodies and silence, a form is merely a guide. So are ideas. The memory of music as great as the music itself.

There are those who say, *there is no next place*. The dream of sex with many partners is man's greatest achievement; that time has gotten by on lies. O, would you look at the time. That's a lot gone by.

I spend my time trying to think of what I can't remember. Something about jets, hung above the runway like a string of lights, waiting to land. The ground rising.

Last Year's Model

Understanding my eye has been a real struggle. When I was a child I pictured god as Abraham Lincoln swinging down from the sky on a very long rope to scoop up my little dead friend. Now it's more complicated.

The sun burns on. Rows of servers in vaults beneath a mountain in Utah make networked memorials to electronic records of people. Che Guevara is my avatar.

All my inner gaze does is make me dizzy. Robbers in my thoughts tell me what to think about big historic shit and my life. *Prefer what's unique to what's beautiful.*

I have this idea, but then I have to make the language. Which is more a reflection of the spirit of the market than anything else. On the palms of my hands are the words, *Love me.*

The Split Ends of My Beard Have Split Ends

My natural instincts are hardly ever right. When I sleep there is a voice in my ear coming through a cheerleader's megaphone in a really bizarre language. I understand fully. The world is out the window. When we wake on the weekends and my wife wants sex, I say, *the furniture is feline, let's just snuggle*. Then I get up to pee. Nothing's as good as you think it is. I'm old enough now to say of my past, *that was a different time, I'm a different person*. What was that noise? Successful ideas spring from great people. There is this music I heard once and if I could just have it with me at all times, there's no telling what I'd do. I'd like very much to speak the way I'm spoken to when I sleep, to have the perfect cheer. I'd also like to live forever among the brilliant colored cups of the tulips, but know how likely that isn't. If you want my advice, get out while you still can.

Lives of the Young and the Tragic

I traveled the south of France in a car with a woman I loved and whose name I can't remember. These were the days of concern with becoming a self. I hadn't yet learned not to care what would happen. Our surroundings were barren and reminded me of home—ploughed fields and rain, narrow roads and wind, though I admit the lavender was beautiful and smelled wonderful, just as I'd been told.

I was unpracticed, and I guess a nice enough person, indiscriminately professing my love for people and things of which I knew nothing. The sheer face of a mountain was everywhere we went. When we came across a young shepherd at rest beneath a tree watching over his flock, his collie frolicking, my discomfort was immense. Never before had I seen such a sight, and never did I want to again, not in reality at least.

In the lowlands, semi-wild horses grazed along the very American looking/feeling highway. Flamingos stood on their skinny legs. Wetland grasses waved in the breeze. The sub-text took the foreground, though it would take me years to learn to call it that, and even longer to realize it had always been there. I couldn't tell if I was genuinely agitated. Everything reminded me of something else, and I got on with things.

Present Whereabouts Unknown

Bulbous, then jack-knifed, the past dots its i's. *Just sit back and enjoy the sun*, the old man used to say. He rarely meant it. The sound of his voice made animals cry. *You will suffer a magnificent failure*, a college girl reading my tarot told me when I was just a freshman.

Now I'm grown. The feast has commenced. Driftwood just misses the large catfish in the corner of the hundred-or-so gallon tank. Four pelicans in formation skim the surf's surface. Everywhere I turn people with hearty names are quaintly smoking.

Elsewhere in America, raccoons tip over garbage cans. Motion detectors make lights come on. Business men and women in meetings fall asleep over their marketing stories. Inspiration's sloppiness. Invention after reinvention. My vagina is a mixed metaphor. When you say talking, you seem to mean complaining. And all I can say is, *Where have I been my whole life?*

Another Year of My Life with Me

Necessity is the mother of my loins. Rarely satisfying. Language, like manners, is inherently depraved. A tingle in the tongue as the earnest multi-instrumentalists double-team the grand piano. I like the way the music makes me move.

*

When I was a child, my father was a goddess. Gender switching was common. Now my boobs keep falling out of my shirt, which really sucks, but if I were into dudes, I'd totally be into you.

*

We can't all be winners, the losers say. My semblables. I tell you, the idea of Hell as an eternity of screaming children is real. Knowing this, what else is there to do but take solace in the secrets rotting beneath the floorboards?

Home Again

Makeshift landmines were all the rage. For reasons beyond my control, people had it in for me, set up mines on a stretch of road close to home, where they knew I'd have to go. Driving, I hit one. A couple tires blew out, the hood flew off. I was going to hit another. So I jumped from my car, which proceeded to blow up.

I found my mother. She was concerned, a little, sent me to live with a family I soon discovered also had it in for me. Their grievances were most likely a result of circumstances beyond my control. They had the same affinity for explosive devices as the people at home, planted them around the house. Their furniture was arranged to limit alternate routes around the mines. They put mines in my bed as I slept. I became adept at never truly sleeping.

Nearing total exhaustion, everything out of focus, I was put in a little room and forced to watch videos of people in the past who had acted like me. The people in the videos were suffering similarly. Landmines were prominently featured. I, however, was faring much better, I thought. Then the room I was in gave way to city streets. Mines were going off all over the place. Another explosion. Then another. Whatever they wanted me to confess, I was almost ready.

False Teeth

I love my teeth—they are really, really white—and fear losing them.

*

I asked my shrink about this when I was in high school. He said, *People who don't look perfect are the sexiest*, but also knew I was a really paranoid and neurotic kid and probably figured that if I found out my fear was legitimate, well, I wouldn't handle it too well.

*

When I was a young tot, I remember brushing my teeth. I was so friggin' happy, and the changes were amazing.

*

As I grew and developed, so did my fascination with teeth and my love for biting. My own teeth were unusual from the beginning. I had too many, and my parents were always on my case. Regardless, I loved my round head.

*

I was Mommy's little girl, and I adored my Daddy. The woman on television said I should just learn to love my teeth for how they were.

*

My grown-up teeth are crooked and my two canine teeth are impacted. I could gnash them and get all frustrated, but that doesn't solve my problem of loving my job but never smiling.

*

Whether I'm brushing my teeth or washing my face or sitting on the big potty, I draw flowers. My teeth feel naked and I have to resist the urge to burn them.

*

The fact that I have no pain because I have no real teeth and there are no root canals expected makes me smile with all of my soul. My love is strong and will float atop my chest forevermore.

Epilogue

Further Down the Purchase Funnel

Fat, bewildered
days stretch into the distance

Music becomes a clatter
         then music again

The end not being accomplished by attainment
so much as being proven to have been attained

long ago

a time when we finally turn
         and see what was there despite our having been there

beautiful human beings
         all

beams of light

         where the bullets entered

photo by Erin Patrice O'Brien

Justin Marks' latest chapbook is *Voir Dire* (Rope-a-Dope Press, 2009). He is the founder and editor of Kitchen Press Chapbooks and lives in New York City with his wife and their infant son and daughter.

The New Issues Poetry Prize

Justin Marks, *A Million in Prizes*
2008 Judge: Carl Phillips

Sandra Beasley, *Theories of Falling*
2007 Judge: Marie Howe

Jason Bredle, *Standing in Line for the Beast*
2006 Judge: Barbara Hamby

Katie Peterson, *This One Tree*
2005 Judge: William Olsen

Kevin Boyle, *A Home for Wayward Girls*
2004 Judge: Rodney Jones

Cynie Cory, *American Girl*
Barbara Maloutas, *In a Combination of Practices*
Louise Mathias, *Lark Apprentice*
Bradley Paul, *The Obvious*
Heidi Lynn (Peppermint) Staples, *Guess Can Gallop*
Ever Saskya, *The Porch is a Journey Different from the House*
Matthew Thorburn, *Subject to Change*
2003 Judge: Brenda Hillman

Paul Guest, *The Resurrection of the Body and the Ruin of the World*
2002 Judge: Campbell McGrath

Sarah Mangold, *Household Mechanics*
2001 Judge: C.D. Wright

Elizabeth Powell, *The Republic of Self*
2000 Judge: C.K. Williams

Joy Manesiotis, *They Sing to Her Bones*
1999 Judge: Marianne Boruch

Malena Mörling, *Ocean Avenue*
1998 Judge: Philip Levine

Marsha de la O, *Black Hope*
1997 Judge: Chase Twichell